Secret Sayings, Hidden Meanings

Practical Wisdom
for a Post-Modern World

by Graham Cooke

The Wisdom Series — Book One

www.BrilliantBookHouse.com

Wisdom that stretches our thinking and enlarges our heart.

A book of aphorisms by Graham Cooke.

Brilliant Book House LLC
865 Cotting Lane, Ste C
Vacaville, California 95688
U.S.A.

www.brilliantbookhouse.com

© 2008 Graham Cooke

All rights reserved. No part of this book may be reproduced, stored in a retrieval system or transmitted in any form or by any means — electronic, mechanical, photocopy, recording, or otherwise — without prior written permission of the copyright owner, except by a reviewer who wishes to quote brief passages in connection with a review for inclusion in a magazine, newspaper or broadcast.

Unless otherwise indicated, all Scripture quotations are taken from The Holy Bible, New King James Version (Copyright © 1979, 1980, 1982 by Thomas Nelson, Inc.) and the New American Standard Bible (Copyright © 1960, 1962, 1963, 1971, 1972, 1973, 1975, 1977, 1995 by The Lockman Foundation).

Requests for information should be addressed to:

Graham Cooke
office@myemerginglight.com

ISBN 978-1-934771-11-2

Cover image by Matt Wolcott and Jared Teska

Dedication

I dedicate this book to my own tribe of friends in Vacaville, California.

I love the way we hang out and do life together. I love the laughter, joking, and the gentle mischief of dear friends.

I love the deep conversations, prayers and wisdom that bind us together in Kingdom purpose.

I love the worship, delight, and deep adoration that is in all our hearts towards the Lord Jesus.

I love the energy, enthusiasm and excitement that the Holy Spirit brings to our corporate journey.

I love the permission that the Father has given us to explore dreams, faith and the land of promise He has opened up to us.

This is the Lord's doing and it is marvelous in our eyes!

Acknowledgements

To all my friends, fellow warriors and co-laborers around the world.

I am grateful for the friends, speakers, songwriters, prophets, apostles and leaders in Asia, Africa, Europe, Australia, Canada, New Zealand, America and the UK... people who have taught me and inspired me, both directly and indirectly, by their lives, words, and example under pressure.

My grateful thanks to mentors now walking the green fields of Paradise, and for current guides who coach me in the ways of the Lord.

A Note on Meditation

The purpose of this book is to lead you out of the busyness of life and into the still waters of deep thought, restful perception and therefore *presence*. As you give yourself to this process you will become more God-conscious, more of a worshipper, and more peaceful in how you approach life.

To meditate means to think deeply about something or someone. It means to explore with mind and heart, allowing what you think to touch your innermost being.

Meditation is creative thought which leads us to the higher realm of revelation and wisdom. It takes us beyond the place of reason to where joy is seated and faith is activated.

Meditation allows us to search inside and outside the box of our current paradigm. What you see and hear there touches you profoundly. It adds a ring around the core truth of Christ which is God within, the certainty of freedom.

Fruitful meditation is therefore not a casual seeking for revelatory insight. Initial creative thoughts are merely the "X" that marks the spot. There is treasure in meditation, a guarantee of wealth in the pursuit of God.

Many are satisfied with collecting random truth on the surface of their consciousness. It is good, wholesome stuff, but it does not satisfy and it cannot challenge the complexities of life in a warfare context.

Deep truth has to be mined over days and weeks. It takes joy and patience to take truth down to its deepest level. Beyond meeting our current needs. Beyond the depth of understanding the power it releases to us against our adversary. Down to the depth where God lives in the highest places of heaven. For all meditation must ultimately come before the throne of His majesty, sovereignty and supremacy. He fills all things with Himself.

Our current situation requires wisdom, but even more it yearns for *Presence*. Meditation allows us to experience both, through the word coming alive in our spirit. Meditation leads us to God and the permission of His heart. Learn to be in the question peacefully with God. Let the Holy Spirit teach you how to abide. Turn inwardly and rest; wait patiently… He will come. When your heart gets restless, turn to worship. When the interior atmosphere settles, return to listening.

Write down initial thoughts but do not pursue them just yet. Do not be distracted by what you hear initially. Set it aside; come back to it later.

When first entering a lifestyle of meditation, take care to ease into it slowly. An hour at first, then longer until half a day and so on.

Always have a focus; do not try to wait in a vacuum. In this book are a series of sayings and life statements. Take time to process them. Enjoy the stillness of deep thinking and allow your heart to flow in and out of worship.

Use the questions as the Spirit leads. They are not prescriptive but merely a guide to enable your contemplation. No doubt you will discover better questions as the Holy Spirit tutors you.

Enjoy!

About Personal Notes

Following every entry, you will find blank or mostly blank pages like this one. Each of these has a question or questions to help direct you in your meditation. They can be used or ignored; they are merely there as a starting point or guide. These "Personal Notes" sections have been included so you may write His thoughts and keep them close.

Dear Reader:
Some of the sayings
in this book are not
explained...
I did not want to deprive
the Holy Spirit of the
joy of sharing His heart
with you... Himself.

If you want to see things you've never seen before... you must be prepared to do things you have never done before!

1

What does this mean for you?

We are always defined by the intentions of God

To do well in the Spirit your heart must be attuned to the purpose of the Father.

His heart and affection for you must govern every facet of your being. To walk in the Spirit is to walk in the acceptance of a loving God who sees you as His much beloved child.

Brilliant fathers have great intentions towards their children. They think ahead and they live with them in the present.

The Father has great plans for you (Jeremiah 29:11). His intentions say a great deal about you and the quality of life He desires to give you.

Prophecy is the future spoken in advance. Dreams and visions open us up to the claims of God. He has designs on you.

You are made for a specific purpose. When you determine that purpose, all the intentionality of God begins to open up to you.

Meditate on prophetic words, dreams, visions or scriptures that God has given you.

What do they say about you? What can you determine of God's intentionality for you?

What impact will these intentions have on your present–future lifestyle?

Personal Notes

Your identity is who you are…
regardless of circumstances

If you come home from work one evening to find your home and all your possessions have been burned to the ground and your wife and children safe but crying… what would you do first?

Probably a dozen things would come to your mind. One of the first aspects of your identity to reassert itself would be The Provider. You would call up the Father in you, hug your wife, cuddle your children and get them to a safe place.

You would make sure they were fed, had a place to sleep, and an environment that would provide safety and security.

Every situation, good or bad, makes a withdrawal on our identity. We demonstrate our Christ-likeness or our carnality. There is no one else to blame for this since we are in charge of who we are and how we show up.

It is not what other people say or do to us that defines our life… it is our response. Jesus is the same towards us yesterday, today and forever. His love for us is unchanging. He certainly does not love us according to our performance, maturity or immaturity.

Whether we do well or badly, He is consistent in His heart toward us. He has a series of internal values that allow Him to be consistent.

Personal Notes

In what way are you inconsistent? Do you give like for like... good and bad? Are you changeable, judgmental, treating people as they treat you?

What would it mean for you to develop a Christ-like consistency towards friend or foe? What would have to change at this time?

Radical renewal
or business as usual?

When push comes to shove, most of us stay the same. We are in love with the idea of change but not the practice of it.

We love to respond to God in meetings. We want impartation. We love the promises and the prophecies of God. All of these impart an anointing to partner with God in all the developments of life.

All of life in the Spirit either comes to us or is established in us by process. If we have an impartation to enter a new place in Christ, then the process that comes is designed to establish that reality. If the Father uses process to cause us to enter a new place in Christ, then an impartation will come to empower us to abide.

Either way, process is a part of the... process! It is a series of steps designed to move us from one reality to another and enable us to complete the journey.

Most impartations are lost somewhere between the altar and the street. We want new, but we think old. We settle back into life as normal, business as usual, both as individuals and as a corporate body.

I have seen numerous churches receive quite amazing prophetic words, but leadership does not enter the process of adjustment so that they can encounter the Lord in the way that He is requiring.

Life in the Spirit is always about the process of becoming more in Jesus. We must partner with God in the process of our transformation.

Love the promises of God. Love the process that enables you to see them fulfilled.

What promises or prophecies have been spoken over your life? Define the process of change that you must encounter as you move into that new reality. Are your current circumstances part of the process of God changing you?

It's gonna rain; sell your umbrella!

Sometimes we unconsciously protect ourselves from an outpouring of God. We demonstrate caution when we should be wholehearted.

We look from the sidelines instead of jumping into the action. We are passive in our worship rather than engaged.

We must never be prudent about the Holy Spirit. There is no discretion when it comes to God. Everything in Him is "Yes! and amen in Christ," towards us.

We need the same response back to Him. When we have a promise of latter rain, former rain; *any* rain... immediately get rid of everything that would prevent you from soaking in His Presence.

Get rid of all inappropriate mindsets and attitudes. It's called humbling yourself. Put yourself in a place to receive. Believe simply; expect hugely.

Personal Notes

What is stopping you from experiencing a fresh encounter with God?

Disempower
your disappointments

Whatever we focus on, we give power to. *"Set your mind on things above, not on things on the earth."* (Colossians 3:2)

We have all had experiences of being hurt, wounded, betrayed and let down. As sure as the sun rises and sets, we will have similar experiences in the future. Life is not about avoiding unpleasant situations. It is about making a profit from them.

What if every potentially damaging situation was really a shortcut to a brilliant experience of Jesus? Instead of being wounded we would become Christ-like! Through His blood and sacrifice we do not have a right to be wounded; we have a right to be healed.

Take your eyes off the negative and you will disempower it. If you are wounded and offended, it proves that your old nature is still alive. The best way to keep it dead is to live in the new nature of "Christ in you, the hope of glory."

Do not treat disappointments as house guests. In the kingdom we attack the negative and we drive it out. It has neither possession nor inheritance with us.

Make a list of your disappointments and evict them from your life. To every disappointment there is an equal and opposite blessing. Determine the blessing and concentrate on that; live in it — put on Christ.

7

The measure of a man
is not how much it
takes to make him
happy... but how little.

Personal Notes

Take time to redefine what makes you happy.

All of life is spiritual

There is no sacred and secular; there is only life in the Spirit. Everything we do and say impacts the realm of the Spirit. We are more when we are concentrating on being alive to God rather than dead to self. We are more focused on being led by the Spirit than trying to avoid certain situations.

The consequence of focus on God is that we do not find ourselves in displeasing circumstances. God created life to be enjoyed. He moves through everything. He is always touching lives, whether they belong to Him or not.

We can see the footprint of His Kingdom in all places. We smell the fragrance of His Presence in lots of situations. When we say that some things are sacred and others are not, we are cutting down the territory that God loves to move in.

He is everywhere. His creativity is unfettered. You will find Him in the same marketplace as the heathen, the atheist and the agnostic. He will put His own music into their world; His own images on their movie screens. He will use all people as well as His own.

He is the King of love and an absorbing inspiration to everyone, everywhere. Please don't assign Him a territory to suit your religious beliefs. Instead, learn the joy of seeing His footprints everywhere. Detect the fragrance of His Presence even on the most surprising of people. It will make your day and it will make Him smile. It's our secret, that we share with Him.

Do not look for evil. Look for the goodness of God all around you.

As you look for signs of His Presence, many more opportunities will occur for you to bless people and share God's true nature.

With whom and where are you going to start this wonderful way of seeing?

For every flow, there is an ebb

We cannot live in a continuous flow of the Spirit. It is not how life in Jesus is defined. What is true in the Spirit is also true in the natural and vice versa.

Life is seasonal. While it does not match the annual calendar of nature, there are times and seasons. Read Ecclesiastes chapter 3. Spiritual life can be tidal. What we gain in the flow must be consolidated in the ebb. The Holy Spirit is still magnificently present, just in a different way.

To grow effectively in ministry, we must be pruned so that more fruit may come. When we are cut back it is always to go deeper in our relationship with Jesus.

We are all a makeup of Mary and Martha. We need both identities at work in us; the issue is, which has precedence? That is solely based on the will of God at the time!

There is no downside to life. Only a better way of viewing what God is allowing. We move with Him. We learn from Him. We stay in Christ.

The secret of learning in the Spirit is to abide in Jesus. As we remain in Him and rejoice, wisdom releases us to live in the moment and develop significance.

Personal Notes

What is your particular season at this time? What is the Father allowing for your development? What is the wisdom you need to process this necessary part of your journey? How will you position yourself before the Holy Spirit?

Pay attention to the wonder of it all

It's possible to go through life and never touch Heaven as much as the Lord would desire you to.

Our spiritual perceptions can be measured in fragments of time and experience. If God never leaves us nor forsakes us, then He is always present. You owe it to yourself to be more aware of His position in your situation.

We must practice focus or lose it. What if there are amazing experiences that you could be having on a regular basis? They do not appear because we pay little attention to the desire and intentionality of God.

Even in difficult times, life should have a certain splendor. God is here... and glory comes with Him. Life in Jesus is more wonderful than we imagine. Lift your head up and ask to see. Learn to look beyond your situation and see the fine hand of God at work.

Pay attention to wonder and you will journey a hundred times better.

Personal Notes

Is your life mundane? Are you merely drifting through each day, sleepwalking through life? Pay attention. He is here. What can you see?

Tension does not mean that something is wrong... it means something is happening!

There is no movement without tension. If you are relaxing at home and you reach for your coffee cup, your hand must tense up in order to grip the handle properly.

What is true in the natural is also true in the Spirit. In order for us to get hold of what God is doing, we must allow a necessary tension in our actions.

Whenever we relate at depth with people, tension is always one of the ingredients. It is important that we can step back from the stress so that tension does not become a friction. All relationships need the oil of the Holy Spirit.

Tension tells us that we are close to something in the purpose of God. Make it a positive experience or lose control to the enemy.

Be excited about tension and then you can ask better questions to determine the purpose of God.

Personal Notes

Tension has a purpose. What is it? Do not view people around you as negative; there is a more valuable perspective. What is it? What can you be excited and encouraged about?

Divine Acceleration

There is a quickening spirit abroad in the earth. The Father is speeding up His timetable. He is redeeming time for us because the days are increasing in wickedness.

He redeems time by speeding up our development. Have you felt the pace of your spirituality and faith increasing? What we think will take years will take months. Months will become weeks as God gears up in our lives. What would normally take weeks will now occur in days, until we learn to be present to the moment with God.

Divine Acceleration will become a normal part of your experience. Say "yes" more quickly. Respond to the process of growth more obediently.

Most of us, hand on heart, know that we are behind the time of our own development. We must run to catch up.

Personal Notes

What is happening at this time? What must you say "yes" to? What is the area of your life that God wants to accelerate? How will you cooperate?

12

The inner man of the spirit must become the anchor man of the soul

We are not governed by externals. We are led by the Spirit. Our soul by itself will control our experiences, but we will go nowhere. Your soul was created as a vehicle for the Spirit. It should have no authority, only obedience. Your soul is made up of your will, your mind and emotions.

Each must come under the rule of the Holy Spirit living in your human spirit. We are born again by the Spirit so that we can experience God within.

When we experience life from an external perspective, we are subject to all the stress and pressure from that realm. When we conduct life from the Spirit, we are vulnerable to the nature of God in the fruit of the Spirit and we are open to faith and His character. Power comes from a life lived within Christ and within ourselves. The soul needs to be anchored in serving the spirit*. Then we are at our most joyful, peaceful and powerful. Our perception of God comes from being renewed in the spirit of our mind so that the mind of Christ empowers us to receive wisdom.

In order to prosper in all our situations, we must live from the inside out.

*For a more detailed understanding, please read Towards a Powerful Inner Life. www.brilliantbookhouse.com.

What does it mean for you to live from within? What current perspectives are driven by external circumstances? How will you cooperate with the Holy Spirit in living from the right place?

Personal Notes

God is consistent... and unpredictable

We always know where we are with God because He never changes. He remains the same towards us even if our life, responses, and obedience fluctuates.

He will always be gracious and merciful because of Jesus. He will always operate in the fruit of the Spirit in His dealings with us.

We seldom will know how he wants to do things. We are learning to be led by the Spirit. Wisdom is the understanding of how God perceives, how He thinks, and how He plans to do things in our life circumstances.

A cursory view of scripture tells us that often He does not do things the same way twice. What worked in one situation will not work in another, even if they are similar.

There is no substitute for trust and being led by the Spirit. It is a moment-by-moment, day-by-day relationship that is being built into you. Take His hand. His character is predictable; His ways are many and varied.

Personal Notes

Learn to relax in the unchanging nature of God. What does He want to be for you at this time*? Settle into the peace of that and rejoice.

What trust is now possible? What are you seeing of His purpose?

*There are some great thoughts and questions in the interactive journal "The Nature of God."

God does not measure success by results, but by the faithfulness that we display

The world is success oriented; the Kingdom defines success differently on some days.

Success can be to remain standing in difficult circumstances, even if they are not resolved. Other people's obedience may be a factor in us achieving a purpose. Some situations are mainly about learning patience, becoming steadfast, and developing trust in the goodness of God.

Ezekiel was sent to a rebellious nation; a hard people who would oppose him all his life. He was to give the word of the Lord constantly to a people who would ignore him, attack him personally, and fail to respond to his ministry.

Israel did not heed his words and eventually went into bondage and exile. How do you measure his success? It lies in the fact that Ezekiel faithfully prophesied the word of the Lord for more than two decades and then went into exile with them.

Personal Notes

We cannot ignore the requirements of patience, steadfast behavior, and faithfulness to God's purpose.

What are you developing in these areas of our life? Are current circumstances about cultivating these necessary characteristics? Explore.

Owning the future starts now

Do not wait for circumstances to improve before you think about your future.

Your future arises out of your present responses. At this moment your behavior could be denying you a future success. Your calling is made sure in your current development.

Personal Notes

What do you want to be when you grow up in Jesus? What do you want to be known for in the kingdom? The characteristics of your choices are cultivated through your intentional cooperation with the Lord... today!

The truth that sets us free is always rooted in proclamation

Sometimes it is not enough to speak truth into our circumstances. We must shout it out. We must become militant in our confession.

Your inner man of the spirit is attached to your vocal chords. Truth must be proclaimed. Firstly, to God in worship. It is a critical part of our rejoicing and giving thanks.

Secondly, we must declare to the enemy the truth of who we are in Christ; and the purpose of God in our present circumstances.

When we hear proclamation, our faith rises and we take hold of promise and purpose. Proclamation is for everyone, introvert and extrovert. Rejoicing has no personality type. It is the inner man of the Spirit rejoicing aloud in the favor of the Father. Introverts must practice proclamation. Extroverts must cultivate contemplation. Your whole man must be in tune with who God is for you.

If we fail in our proclamation, our victory may be less than we require. The measure that we give ourselves to in responding to God is the limit we set for our breakthrough.

Always, always go the extra mile in obedience.

Personal Notes

Are you an introvert or extrovert? What do you need to do to overcome your personal reticence in proclamation?

What proclamation does the Holy Spirit most want to put into your mouth at this time?

17

18

The Holy Spirit is incredibly enthusiastic about you!

Ask Him to reveal that part of His nature to you. What would it mean for you to see Him in this way? How would it change your relationship with Him? How does it affect you in your current circumstances?

Many people are unequally yoked to a negative

When we learn rest we become more yoked to Jesus in partnership (Matthew chapter 11).

If our normal tendency is to think from a negative mindset, we need to repent and think again. Worry, anxiety, fear, anger, bitterness and resentment will not enable us to become Christ-like.

A successful relationship with Jesus is founded on rest, peace, trust, faith and worship. It yokes us to a positive renewal in our thinking and we are transformed in our lifestyle.

Personal Notes

Is it easier for you to think from a negative perspective? What must you do to change that outlook?

Don't pretend… Practice

Talking to a friend one day who was struggling with his relationship to another person, I shared about the need to love as a first requirement.

This clearly bothered him and he was exasperated with me and defensive about his own actions. We can never justify un-Christlike behavior. When I gently pressed him on his perspective, his explosive reply was "I can't pretend to love him, that's unreality!"

God does not ask us to pretend. He asks us to live in Jesus and practice His nature with the help of the Holy Spirit.

I find it odd that Christians will spend hours praying for the Presence of God to come. He is here. He is within us. Difficult people are our shortcut to becoming Christ-like. They present us with a brilliant opportunity to practice love.

Love your enemies, bless those who persecute you, pray for those who abuse you. It's the only fast track we have to a brilliant relationship with God.

Personal Notes

Who are the hard to love people around you at this time? Identify them and also what they need to see about the goodness and kindness of God. Supply that need! Don't let their lifestyle put you off your own behavior. You are responsible for who you are and how you show up.

Keep a record of what happens as you practice love.

What is the price of not moving on?

When we allow events to stop us from growing, changing and receiving, then we are beating ourselves twice.

Firstly, there is no present victory and secondly, we are denied our future inheritance. Heads the devil wins and tails you lose!

Personal Notes

What are you going to do about it?

In normal circumstances, anxiety is tiring

Check yourself out. What level of peace, joy and laughter is in your life at this time? How much energy, faith and passion are you walking in?

Tiredness, weariness and doubt can all lead us to a place where we live under our circumstances instead of above them.

We can unconsciously slip into a negative state of mind that affects us emotionally and physically.

Look around you at the people who are hard to be with relationally. What are the visible factors at work in them? What is the root cause of their weariness?

Personal Notes

How do you plan to extricate yourself from that condition? What can you be to someone who has allowed weariness to affect their personality?

In Christ we have a delegated authority to destroy the works of the devil!

How's that workin' out for ya? What is the next place in your life where you must develop authority in Jesus?

The gifts of God must be contended for in life

Gifts are freely given in the kingdom. However, they only remain with us at a low level of power.

Personal discipline increases power. What is true for an athlete is true for a minister. The training makes us fit to contend effectively. Gifts grow by use. The intimacy that surrounds each gift is important to understand and experience.

Prophecy requires a knowing of God's heart. It demands an experience of His nature. We must be changed by the heart of God before we can become a representative of it.

As we discipline ourselves in the use of the gifts, the anointing on them increases. In the case of prophecy, your relational experience of God must always be out in front of your prophetic gift. Sadly, I know too many people whose prophetic ability after twenty years is still only at a minor level. The Father trusts what we are manifesting of the Son.

Personal Notes

What is your spiritual gift? What is the required intimacy for moving in that gift at a higher level?

What discipline does your life require for the gift and calling God has purposed over you?

There is no freedom outside of rest

Without rest we are bound. We are prone to worry, anxiety, and fear. Our anger, bitterness and resentment will get the better of us.

Rest allows us space to be. Inner space is freedom to perceive a thing as God sees it. Rest is a prelude to focus. Focus is the forerunner of faith.

When we have no personal discipline of rest and peace, we are seriously behind in terms of our development. Rest allows us to see into the spirit. It creates an expectancy in our hearts and empowers our intimacy.

We must labor to enter into rest (Hebrews 4:11) — we work at resting! We push away anything that would cause worry, anxiety, fear. We do not speculate negatively but we believe the best of the Father. Rest requires a foundation of rejoicing and giving of thanks.

You are at rest, now, in Jesus. Abide in Him. Stay at rest. We do not work hard to acquire rest. It is freely given. We work hard to remain in it.

Personal Notes

What does your rest and peace look like? When was the last time you upgraded it? How strong is the partnership between rest and rejoicing in your life?

Rejoice in who you are...
and in who you are becoming!

Our relationship with God is always present–future in nature. He loves who we are now; He sees the emerging us that is coming to meet us from the future.

Jesus was fond of saying: "An hour is coming and now is…" (John 4:23) highlighting the relationship between present and future that makes our spirituality prophetic in nature.

Give thanks for what God has done in you. Rejoice in where you are now by His grace. Look forward to more of His goodness for your future. "God is working in you to will and to do His good pleasure." (Philippians 2:13)

Your testimony of what God has done for you and Who He is for you are most critical in your intimacy with Him. There is a better version of you coming! Enjoy who you are now.

Personal Notes

Journal what that means for you. Develop a stronger perspective on your present–future relationship with the Father.

27

What you see for yourself in the face of God... you will reflect back to Him.

What are you seeing? What does that mean for you in your present circumstances? How will you reflect it back?

Personal Notes

Opposition attaches to what you don't remove

In order to give us a brilliant future, the Father must eradicate our past. When we do not cooperate fully in the present, we leave gaps in our obedience that the enemy will exploit.

Are you holding onto grudges, offenses and betrayals? When you think of people who have wounded you, is there still resentment, bitterness, or a desire to be vindicated or proven right? How strong are those thoughts and emotions?

If you are harboring unhealthy feelings then the enemy is still beating you up. What joy for him to prevent you from moving on in the Spirit. How much pleasure you give him by not experiencing God fully. Imagine how delighted he will be if your woundedness cripples someone else besides you. If your freedom is not full then maybe the enemy is still linked to you.

Personal Notes

What are you going to do about that? The antidote is forgiveness; blessing other people and renouncing your own disobedience.

Demoralization is a strategic attack against your morale

Demoralize... (dictionary definition)	To corrupt morally; to lower the morale of someone; to deprive people of spirit and confidence; to throw into confusion; to divert someone from a chosen path; to undermine an identity.
Demoralize... (Thesaurus)	To cripple; daunt; deject; depress; dishearten; enfeeble; rattle; undermine; weaken.
Opposite Spirit:	To boost; cheer; comfort; encourage; hearten; inspire; reassure; support; increase; strengthen; uplift; favor; prosper; enlighten.

Personal Notes

Partner with the Holy Spirit or empower the enemy? Your choice.

29

The enemy is measuring
you for a coffin... God
is measuring you for
an ongoing move
of the Spirit.

30

Personal Notes

What is the Father lining you up for in this season?

You are responsible for your own spirituality

There is no-one else to blame. The Lord is in you and you have the joyful enterprise of learning to abide in Him. (John chapter 15)

When we make someone else responsible for our development, we cease to be obedient. We forfeit faith and we lose out on the chief part of our delight… being led by the Spirit.

We hand over all our benefits of loving relationship and we start to live on spiritual welfare. We become poor in spirit.

Personal Notes

If you are in that place, read Matthew 5:3. What blessing awaits you now? What is the Father planning to give you at this time?

At the very, very least, you are always ankle deep in blessing!

The Father never allows us to be without blessing. Often, we miss the numerous small blessings, favor and encouragements that swirl around our life every day.

We have a permanent place in the shallows of His loving-kindness and grace. He always displays His generous love to us. Having our needs met in Jesus is to live in the shallows. That is the very *least* of our good fortune. You have enough favor to overcome what the enemy is doing, since only a small part of God's grace is needed for him to be defeated.

Personal Notes

Why not simply move on? Further in and further up. Your real inheritance is waiting!

32

See your life as a contribution

"Give and it shall be given you. They will pour into your lap a good measure, pressed down, shaken together, and running over. For by your standard of measure it will be measured to you in return." Luke 6:38

We always give our way into our blessing and our future. Being a contribution to everyone you meet means that you attract blessing and favor constantly.

You will always be blessed, encouraged and favored. It's a no-brainer!

Personal Notes

Change your mindset and change your future.

What do you have to give? Who are you going to bless first? Keep a journal of blessings bestowed and favor received. It's exciting.

Personal Notes

34

When in conflict with someone, allow the Holy Spirit to create in you the right spirit to deal with the problem. Then establish the correct development process to empower the other person.

What you give to others always empowers you. It's the process that makes you rich.

Journal your way into a deeper place of your identity and inheritance by using conflict properly.

Faith does not procrastinate

Faith is living and active. It should match the relationship that we have with the Father.

It is our privilege to be confident and assured in His Name and Nature. Faith steps out onto the ground of God's identity. He is worthy of trust.

Faith never hangs back. It climbs out of the boat at the smallest invitation. The only time that faith takes time to produce something is when the Lord teams it with patience. Faith and patience will always inherit eventually. There is usually a "now" quality to faith — a stepping into something by permission.

We never look at what we are stepping onto or into with faith. We look at the nature of the permission. What God permits, He supports us in.

Do not wait to believe. Unless the Lord says otherwise, believe now! Faith is always immediate unless there are other instructions. Do it now!

35

Personal Notes

What do you need to believe God for at this time? What permission(s) do you have already? What prophecies or promises have already been spoken over your life? Don't wait... act!

36

It is not your job to change people... only to demonstrate what God is really like.

Think of the people around you. What does the Lord want to be for them now? What confidence, encouragement and assurance do they need in order to step up into a new level or place with God?

Over to you... that's your role at this time. Make notes on your family and friends, then go and be the gift that the Father wants you to be.

You are either the obstacle or the catalyst for real change to occur

Do you want to be part of the problem or part of the solution? How many times has your resistance prevented something from happening? How often has your obedience created an opportunity?

You are a catalyst; a door opener; one who creates breakthrough. God can trust you to stand when others run. He can expect you to see things that others do not.

You are not ordinary, you are exceptional. Your passion causes you to press into God. You are an explorer of God's nature. What you have discovered about the Lord will make you strong enough to do exploits.

If you were an obstacle to God, how would people describe you? If you were a catalyst for the power of the Holy Spirit, what would that look like? Do the exercise; at least you'll know what to avoid and what to become.

Unlearning is as much fun as the learning of new things

We learn retrospectively as much as we do in the moment. We are always changing, becoming more in our identity.

In our prior persona we were sure about so many things. As we change and become more like Jesus some of these old thoughts and paradigms pass away and new things emerge. Our experiences of God are defined by different truths that we did not know before.

We get to unlearn. It is important to lay aside perceptions when they become inappropriate or inaccurate. A friend of mine grew up as a cessationist, not believing in the person and work of the Holy Spirit as a modern day relational experience. Most of his relationship with God was cerebral, logical and without passion.

It was a massive shock to him to discover that the Holy Spirit is a real, tangible person with the most amazing and fabulous identity and personality.

Watching my friend unlearn the lie about the Holy Spirit was a fascinating part of our journey of friendship. The joy given to him by the Father was outstanding. Watching another of my friends, who came from a "word" church, discover worship for herself was brilliant fun. She came into a deeply joyful place of rejoicing and praise… it changed her entire personality!

There is no condemnation. That thought alone makes the unlearning enjoyable.

Do not just discard your unlearning but process it properly in your heart and mind. Know not only *what* you are giving up, but *why*. Then, what you replace it with will guarantee a great experience. What are you unlearning?

He is all-consuming life and the power of Him makes our puny heart feel like a fortress that cannot be taken

How glorious it is to simply rest in majesty. To relax into the immensity of God. He fills everything with Himself.

He loves you. He loves you with all of His heart, soul, mind and strength. He loves you in the same way that He requires love from you. The difference is that He *supplies* you with the love that He desires *from* you.

To feel the strength of God's love in the weakest place of your heart and in a powerless moment is an amazing experience. Even better, though, is to know that you can expect God to be there for you in that way, and that you can wait joyfully for His love to touch you.

In your weakest moment you are powerfully loved. That love overpowers all that you are not. It overwhelms all your inadequacy. It empowers you to stand up on the inside. Love makes us invincible, unbeatable. Our heart becomes a fortress. Only God can do that… turn a weak place into something impregnable.

39

Meditate on that. Ask the Father to show you what that process would look and feel like. Journal your thoughts.

Our boldness in coming to God and our sense of expectation will be a huge inspiration to others

The one who believes in Jesus shall not be disappointed (Romans 9:33). The Holy Spirit is our tutor to school us into becoming like Jesus.

On earth Jesus was not God pretending to be a man. He really was a man, living in right relationship with the Father. Therefore, He models to His people the right attitude and approach to God.

His relationship with the Father gave the watching people an opportunity to see and believe (John 11:41–43). Now that we are in Christ, this is our life too!

Look at your life now. Where is the first place you get to practice boldness and confidence?

It's hard work being out of sync with the Father!

We are in Jesus. We have been put in this place by the Father as a gift. We need to do nothing to get there; we are in. We abide by agreement. We experience the power of that union through our obedience to stay, dwell and remain. We can do nothing to enter this place; we must do everything to remain here.

Being in Christ is the Father's gift to us; staying in Christ is our gift to Him. He has made being in Christ a delight. We now share a restful, joyful rhythm and harmony. Our peace is the evidence that we are abiding correctly. All is rest. Everything contains joy. It is a simple and powerful life that we have been given. Staying in Christ is so much easier than being out of sync with God.

Outside of God we are prone to depression, weariness, anxiety, fears and doubts. That is *hard work*!! … and for no reward or benefit. Not to abide in Christ, in a dark world, is extreme foolishness.

Personal Notes

Write an honest account regarding the status of your relationship with the Father in Christ. What would you change first?

Personal Notes

The intimacy of being hidden in Christ before the enemy maintains our loving relationship with God in times of conflict.

42

Personal Notes

Meditate on that statement and journal the revelation you receive.

Within that revelation you will discover an inheritance word for your next season.

We can wear down the enemy by our freshness

"Though our outer man (of the body) is decaying, yet our inner man (of the spirit) is being renewed day by day." (2 Corinthians 4:16)

"'The Lord's loving-kindnesses indeed never cease for His compassions never fail. They are new every morning. Great is Your Faithfulness. The Lord is my portion, says my soul. Therefore I have hope in Him." (Lamentations 3:22-24)

Every day we start afresh in God's love. We carry over no negative into the next dawn. When the sun rises fresh to greet the day, so do we. It suits the enemy for us never to discover freshness as a way of life. Because he has no access to God's abundance, the devil is weary. All he can do is try to make everyone as he is himself. Weighed down, burdened, angry, resentful, and bitter.

We live in daylight compartments. We live, one day at a time. The mindset with which you begin each day will support your next experience of either God or the enemy.

Identify the places of weariness in your life where your experience of God has become stale. How will the Holy Spirit freshen you up? What do you need to do to stay fresher, longer?

A crisis attracts the power and the strength of God

On the pathway of your life, the Father knows where every attack, every crisis, and every problem is located.

Next to each difficulty He has placed a promise and a provision. When we locate the tribulation, we uncover the revelation that is also present.

We stand on the promise looking at the provision and we rejoice! As we "count it all joy," (James 1:2) the truth becomes our experience and we are set free.

Personal Notes

Look at your present difficulty. What is the promise? Where is the provision? When you locate them, you will discover the Lord. He will be the One that is smiling.

We can tell the quality of someone's inner life by the amount of opposition it takes to discourage them

If we are growing up in all things in Christ, the enemy will have to work harder against us this year than last. The enemy uses intimidation because it's cheap. Only God is infinite and only He has abundance. The enemy has a budget. The devil has to calculate everything. How can he achieve huge gains with the least expenditure of resources? That's easy: put the frighteners on Christians by using intimidation. It worked for Goliath against all the soldiers of Israel. Then he met a warrior who practiced intimacy and he lost his head.

Real Christians bear weight. They are strong enough to carry the heaviness of the anointing of the Spirit. The heavier the substance of your anointing, the more resources the enemy must deploy to counter your influence in the earth. The stronger the attack against you, the more Presence God commits to you. What a great life we have!

If we do not abide in Christ, we have no substance. We are easily distracted, intimidated and overcome. We are poor in spirit. Even here at the low place of our experience, the Father has placed a blessing (Matthew 5:30) so that we can begin to recover who we really are in Jesus. "As He is, so are we, in this world." (1 John 4:17)

We always choose our experience. To be overcome or to be an overcomer? When crises happen around your life, family and friends, who are you in the context of that? What comes out of your heart in those moments? This is where your quality is defined.

45

To grow in substance in the anointing, you need a revelation of Jesus greater than your perspective on the situation at hand.

Who is Jesus for you right now? What blessing and anointing is present in your circumstances? Journal what it means for you to put off the old nature and put on the new!

Make sure the Holy Spirit has enough room to move

Doubt, fear and unbelief closes down the operation of God (Matthew 13:58). God loves to create a climate of faith; the enemy, one of unbelief.

The Father stimulates, the devil debilitates. We must open ourselves up to who God is for us. The best and most consistent way to do that is by rejoicing, giving thanks and joyful praying. (1 Thessalonians 5:16–18 & Philippians 4:6)

We are always in partnership with someone! (Joshua 24:15) Your choice of partner dictates your success.

Personal Notes

Ask the Holy Spirit to create a clearing in your situation, i.e., a space for you to breathe and refocus.

What are you seeing now? Open your heart as fully as you are able... then continue. Be stretched by the goodness of God. Now read Psalm 27:13 and meditate on it. What truth is present to arm you in your situation?

47

Champions are not made
in the ring... they are
only recognized there.

Does your training fit your calling?

What is the difference between your training ground and your proving ground?

48

Your truest identity is composed of your personality and your persona

When Jesus asked the question, "Who do you say that I am?" (Matthew 16:15), he was not fishing for compliments. He was leading up to a crucial point regarding identity.

When you know who you are then you know how you are supposed to live, both within yourself and towards the people around you. When they know your real identity, then they must act accordingly towards you.

He wanted the disciples to understand His true identity because that revelation would shape their relationship. We get to live out our truest identity before family, friends and others in a way that supports relationships and the journey we are on together.

My two passions (after Jesus) are wisdom and prophecy. I am known far and wide as a wise teacher and as a prophet. People know that I will only speak what God is speaking, without fear or favoritism. They know that if God is silent on a matter, then I cannot be pressured into talking. This is my persona. It is me stepping into my calling and gifting. It is my public face that the Father displays by His approval and anointing.

There is a difference between our personality and our persona. My personality is that of a hard working, fairly quiet English guy who is a loyal friend, deep thinker and always ready for some fun, if not a little mischief. Persona and personality are two sides of the same coin. Together they make up the sum total of our truest identity. They are both relational and functional. It is a paradox. We are relational and functional in both areas. The point about paradox is *what has precedence*. That is mostly decided by circumstances and the need of the moment.

My family does not need a prophet to show up all the time, nor do my friends! Similarly, when I am on tour, people need Graham to show up within the scope of his calling as well as his personality.

When God initially shows up in our life and calls us to a specific task, He is introducing us to our persona as He defines it. We meet His calling in our personality, because at that time it is all we have. Our personality is never equal to the task. Initially we make excuses because we are undeveloped in our truest identity.

Gideon was hiding out from the Midianites, threshing wheat in a wine press (Judges chapter 6). When God showed up He immediately spoke to Gideon's persona, calling him a "valiant warrior and a deliverer who has strength." What followed is the usual pattern of behavior when a person is faced up to the other part of their identity. The fleece that Gideon laid before God was not about guidance, it was about reassurance. Gideon needed confidence about his persona: "If you will deliver Israel through me, as you have spoken." He needed a sign that his persona was valid.

Moses faced a similar internal battle when God called him to deliver Israel from bondage (Exodus 3:10–12). He met the call in his personality and was unequal to it. A part of us has to grow up in our relationship with God. Moses had to "see" who he was in this next season of his life (Exodus 7:1). If we do not see our persona, we cannot develop our truest identity. Also, if the people around us do not see our truest identity, then it is hard for us to accomplish anything with them.

When Jesus asked "Who do you say I am?", He was looking to see if they perceived His persona. When Simon spoke out "You are the Christ, the Son of the Living God," something shifted in the heavens.

In that moment Simon's own persona was revealed to him and the others listening (Matthew 16:17–19): "You are Peter, and you will have keys to bind and loose. The revelation you perceive shall be the bedrock of the church and hell will be defeated by it."

Personal Notes

What is your personality? Define it, measure it, and record it.

What is your calling and vision? Journal your uniqueness on this page.

How will you step into your truest identity with God and man?

Journal the help, support and development you will need from the Lord. (Exodus 3:12)

Stepping Into Your Truest Identity is available on CD on the Brilliant Book House website.

Failure is less traumatic than regret

Failure is not to be feared. We cannot win if we are afraid to lose. It takes real courage to try something when the odds are against you succeeding.

A renewed mind and an enlightened heart will both face life positively. They are both confident in the grace and goodness of God.

It is much better to try and to fail than never have the courage to go after something. Too many missed opportunities lead us into the valley of shadow, where we are a pale version of what we could have been. Passivity, procrastination and caution are all forms of regret. It is where we look back at our fainthearted approach to life and discover how timid we have become.

The future is still stretching before us. It is vital that our past does not become our future or regret will shadow us all our lives.

Be honest. What part has fear played in your life? Perhaps you call it caution and turn it into something of a virtue? Are you always tentative? How often are you confident? Have you ever been bold? If you are no longer going to live with regret, what do you need to do at this point in your life?

Write out a realistic appraisal of your caution, confidence and boldness. If you feel more fear than confidence, then fear has a hold on you. If you always require assurance, then confidence is not yet a part of your nature. What are you going to do about that?

Love without trust is nothing

50

If we love God with all our heart, soul, mind and strength, then we must trust Him in the same way.

At the very, very least, that means we must banish negativity in our minds and hearts. At the very best it means that we are capable of incredible acts of faith in the power of the spirit.

Only God can love God properly. His love for us embraces all that we are (as well as all that we are not) and enfolds us in all that He is towards us.

We trust in the context of how much we are loved. He who is forgiven much, loves much. Or to put it another way, when you are totally loved you can experience forgiveness to the greatest depth.

Either way, love and forgiveness are closely linked. So too are love and trust. Let God love you. That's your daily delight. Partner with the Holy Spirit in the act of being the Beloved.

Faith is best expressed in the context of love. Don't try to trust; instead, allow yourself to be loved. As you experience love, your confidence will rise in terms of how you believe God sees you. Confidence only has to rise a fraction to reveal trust. Actually your inner man is waiting to trust God. The love of God causes the inner man to rise up above the soul.

In this love, we discover His nature. When we know what the Father is really, really like… we relax in Him. We trust as a much-loved child. Our father is incredible and we depend on Him totally. That's a good place to start each day.

You are wonderfully loved. Rest in that. Relax in Him and trust will be present. Trust is the evidence of love. You cannot be anxious, worried or fearful if you are perfectly loved. Perfect love casts our fear. (1 John 4:18)

Love and trust combine to take us into new and exciting levels of experience. There are adventures that can begin when we allow these two aspects of God's nature to come together in our hearts.

When they combine consistently, we can never be negative, nor cautious. Instead of being cautious, we are curious. What will the

Father do? What is the Holy Spirit teaching me? What is my position in Jesus?

We are not negative about life; we are excited about Jesus. We are in Him and He is in us. Therefore, life is full of wonderful possibilities. In the love of God we trust Him for every one of them.

Personal Notes

The love of God comes to you in the same way that the weather does each day. It is unbidden and ever-present.

What would it look like for you to relax and simply embrace each day in the affection of God?

When you are touched by love, express your gratitude in the form of a trust statement. What do you need to trust God for at this time? Love is present so that you may believe.

Practice thinking with all your heart. (Proverbs 3:5–6)

Journal your experience.

Personal Notes

51

What your soul thinks
is a crisis, your inner
man perceives as
an opportunity.

How can you prevent yourself from processing your life through a negative?

What will it take for you to rethink your current difficulties into a place where you can connect with the fullness of God's nature for you?

If difficulties represent opportunities, what blessing, favor and provision awaits you right now?

How will you engage your trust in God with your newfound permission?

Personal Notes

Reclaim your inner
territory as a place of joy

Scripture contains numerous commands for us to rejoice. Giving thanks is good for us. The culture of heaven is founded on celebration. All heaven rejoices in the Presence of God. Joy is the nature of the Father and the chief element in the environment around His throne.

Joy is a necessity. Its power cannot be overestimated. It is a delightfully contagious way to live. God is happy. We live daily under His smile. He is a delight to us. As we learn to be thrilled by Him our own enjoyment of life increases.

We cannot afford to be without joy. The view of life we receive in joy is our best aid to faith. The joyless areas of our heart and daily routine must be subjected to fierce examination. All negative emotions are temporary. Joy is a permanent condition. Return to joy with the utmost urgency.

52

What is standing between you and rejoicing as a lifestyle?

In what way will joy release to you a greater revelation of the love of God?

An Appeal: Anti-Human Trafficking

William Wilberforce has long been one of my favorite heroes. He fought his own government and high society in an epic battle to abolish slavery. He succeeded admirably. In 1833, the British Parliament passed the Slavery Abolition Act which gave freedom to all slaves in the British Empire. Three decades later it also became law in the 13th Amendment to the U.S. Constitution.

Today slavery is back and worse than ever. The U.S. Secretary of State, Condoleeza Rice, states that, "defeating human trafficking is a great moral calling of our time." It is a huge business, profitable to the tune of over $30 billion. Almost 30 million people are enslaved by it. Most are children; millions are sex slaves.

We need to raise up a new generation of abolitionists that can counter a worldwide epidemic. Human trafficking is a criminal enterprise that is international. It is sophisticated in its corruptive influence on law enforcement and government officials across the globe.

More slaves are in bondage today than were sold in 400 years of the slave trade that was abolished in the 1800's. Slaves are disposable people — like batteries: once they exhaust their usefulness, they are replaced.

What is required is a relentless pursuit of justice — a refusal to accept a world where one individual can be held as the property of another. For more than three decades I have financed projects around the world aimed at relieving suffering and creating a better quality of life. Fighting against human trafficking is different. It is not a project; it's more of a crusade. I want to affect things at a high level as well as on the ground.

I have a separate account within the ministry where I am setting aside a percentage of profits from all our endeavors to give into this worthy cause. Join us as the Lord leads you, or get involved some way yourself. Do something!

If you wish to donate with your order through Brilliant Book House (please be advised that we are a for-profit company), then send your gift with the notation "Not For Sale" to:

Brilliant Book House
865 Cotting Ln, Ste C
Vacaville, CA 95688

Alternatively, if you want a tax credit for your gift, more information and a chance to donate can be found at this website: www.notforsalecampaign.org.
Checks can be made payable to Not for Sale:

270 Capistrano Road
Suite #2
Half Moon Bay, CA 94019

Phone: (650) 560-9990
www.notforsalecampaign.org

With heartfelt thanks,
Graham Cooke

Other Books by Graham Cooke

About the Author

Graham Cooke is part of The Mission's core leadership team, working with senior team leader, David Crone, in Vacaville, California. Graham's role includes training, consulting, mentoring and being part of a think tank that examines the journey from present to future.

He is married to Theresa, who has a passion for worship and dance. She loves to be involved in intercession, warfare, and setting people free. She cares about injustice and abuse, and has compassion on people who are sick, suffering and disenfranchised.

They have six children and three grandchildren. Ben and Seth both reside and work in the UK. Ben is developing as a writer, is very funny, and probably knows every movie ever made. Seth is a musician, a deep thinker with a caring outlook and an amazing capacity for mischief. Seth is married to Sara, a lovable, intelligent and very funny girl.

Sophie and her husband Mark live in Vacaville and attend The Mission. Sophie & Mark are the Operations Managers of Brilliant Book House, the publishing company of Graham Cooke. Sophie has played a significant part in Graham's ministry for a number of years, and has helped develop resources, new books and journals, as well as organize events. Mark and Sophie are a warm-hearted, friendly, deeply humorous couple with lots of friends. Mark and Sophie have two daughters. Evelyn (August 2006) is a delight; a happy little soul who likes music, loves to dance and enjoys books. Annabelle (December 2008) is loud, funny, determined and unafraid. Granddaughter #3 is due any day and the name is a secret.

Their other daughters are Alexis, who is loving, kind and gentle, and very intuitive and steadfast toward her friends; and Alyssa, a very focused and determined young woman who is fun-loving with a witty sense of humor.

Also, Graham and Theresa have two beautiful young women, Julianne and Megan, both in Australia, who are a part of their extended family.

Graham is a popular conference speaker and is well known for his training programs on the prophetic, spiritual warfare, intimacy and devotional life, leadership, spirituality and the church in transition. He functions as a consultant and freethinker to businesses, churches, and organizations, enabling them to develop strategically. He has a passion to establish the Kingdom and build prototype churches that can fully reach a post-modern society.

A strong part of Graham's ministry is in producing finances and resources to the poor and disenfranchised in developing countries. He supports many projects specifically for widows, orphans and people in the penal system. He hates abuse of women and works actively against human trafficking and the sex slave trade, including women caught up in prostitution and pornography.

If you would like to invite Graham to minister or speak at an event, please complete the online Ministry Invitation Form at www.GrahamCooke.com.

If you wish to become a financial partner for the sake of missions and compassionate acts across the nations, please contact his office at office@myemerginglight.com, and his administrative assistant will be happy to assist you.

You may contact Graham by writing to:
Graham Cooke
865 Cotting Lane, Ste C
Vacaville, California
95688, USA

www.GrahamCooke.com

Brilliant Book House

Brilliant Book House is a California-based publishing company founded and directed by Graham Cooke and is dedicated to producing high-quality Christian resources and teaching materials. Brilliant Book House seeks to equip all of our readers to lead brilliant lives, confidently led by the Holy Spirit into the destiny God has for you.

We believe you have a unique call on your life that can only be found in God. He has something for you that is far beyond your wildest dreams. As you step out into that purpose, we want to stand with you, offering you encouragement, training, and hope for your journey. We want to equip you for what God wants to do in you, and through you. That is our promise to you.

Brilliant is the culmination of a longtime dream of our founder, Graham Cooke. A thinker and a strategist, Graham is also a builder with a particular desire to establish resource churches that are prophetic, progressive, and supernatural. Brilliant Book House is a key part of that call, producing books, journals, MP3s, e-books, DVDs, CDs, and other teaching materials. For more on Graham, please visit www.brilliantbookhouse.com.